Also by Roger Weingarten

What Are Birds Worth
Ethan Benjamin Boldt

The Vermont Suicides

The Vermont Suicides

Roger Weingarten

Alfred A. Knopf   New York   1978

THIS IS A BORZOI BOOK
PUBLISHED BY ALFRED A. KNOPF, INC.

Copyright © 1977, 1978 by Roger Weingarten
All rights reserved under International and Pan-American Copyright
Conventions. Published in the United States by Alfred A. Knopf, Inc.,
New York, and simultaneously in Canada by Random House of Canada
Limited, Toronto. Distributed by Random House, Inc., New York.

The author wishes to acknowledge his father, Myer Weingarten, Barry and Lorry
Goldensohn, Norman Dubie, Pamela Stewart, and Dina Yellen for their
encouragement during the writing of this book.
Part of this book was written while on an individual artist's grant from
the Vermont Council for the Arts.

Thanks are due to *The Mississippi Review* in which "The Flight of the Stonecutter,"
"The Vermont Suicides," and "Magnetic Waters" first appeared, and to *The Seneca
Review* for their publication of "The Tale of the Green Rose."

Manufactured in the United States of America
First Edition

For Dina

I wish to dedicate certain poems as follows:

The Flight of the Stonecutter
    to Norman Dubie and Pamela Stewart

Costumes in the Forbidden City
    to Marvin and Jill Fisher

Waltzing Roger's Vision
    to my mother, Shirley Weingarten,
    and to my sister and brother,
    Wendy Weingarten and Jeffrey Weingarten

The Vermont Suicides
    to Steven Korshak and Daniel Beavin

The Tale of the Green Rose
    to my grandmother, Ida Sommers.

Contents

The Vermont Suicides

The Tale of the Green Rose

The Flight
of the Stonecutter

The Flight of the Stonecutter

I   Indictment in Marble

Be it remembered, that
at a term of the Honorable
County Court begun and held at Marble
within and for the County of Windsor
on the first Tuesday after the first
Monday in September, in the year of our Lord
one thousand nine hundred four, the Grand Jurors
within and for the body
of the County of Windsor
aforesaid, now here in court duly
impaneled and sworn,
and upon their oath present
their bill of indictment against
Alessandro Garetto, charging
that on the second day of October, in the year
of our Lord one thousand nine hundred four,
with force and arms in and upon
the body of Elia Corti, otherwise called Eli,
of the city of Granite, feloniously,
wilfully, and of his premeditated
malice aforethought, an assault did make
and that the said
Garetto, a certain pistol,
that is to say a revolver, then and there charged
with powder and one
leaden bullet,

which said pistol he the said
Garetto, in his right hand then and there
had and held, then and there feloniously
wilfully, and of his deliberate
malice aforethought, did discharge
and shoot off against the said
Elia Corti, and that
Garetto, with the leaden
bullet aforesaid, out of the pistol aforesaid,
that is to say, the revolver aforesaid, then and there
by the force of gunpowder, then and there feloniously,
wilfully, and of his deliberate
malice aforethought,
discharged, shot off, and did strike,
penetrate, and wound him,
in and upon the right side of the belly
of him, otherwise
called Eli, giving him —as a child
who carved soft
marble finches and a white rose, held
a claw tool and the attention of the master
carvers of the Brera Academy, who pinned silver
and gold medals on his lapels, and believed the sun
would rise on a new century, over ivy-
embroidered fountains: water
over muscle, knotted and climbing
up the gold-veined back of heroic sculpture.
Apprenticed to the trade, he boarded
a ship and with Malena, who tended his fever
and accepted his dish of orange
Venetian glass, with its clear twig-shaped
twisted handle, who told him
the Vermont granite was like its winter,

hard to cut, and if you lived through
albino February and blind March,
you would take your own life in April. At twenty-three
he married, built a home
for the sun, a girl of sixteen, dreaming of an artist
whose hands would shape the intricate
frostcarving on the morning windows, and touch
the children's eyes: Lelia, who recollects
that she was recuperating from an American sickness,
her grandparents caring for her in northern Italy,
wearing a cape of white wool, and playing ring-
around-the-rosy when the news came that tore her life
from Emma, posing in Elia's lap for a family portrait,
who put her down and drew little Mary close to the wax
tips of his moustache, to the cloth-covered
buttons of his three-piece suit, then
Emma cried, he stroked her hair, and seventy years
after that she still feels him assuring her
"I'm here. I'm here." Telling her, a few weeks later
in the hospital bedroom, to put out her hands,
hands that would be touched by the speakable
horrors of world war, telling her to put out her hands
and reach down in her brass-and-leather chest
for the newspaper photographs of his granite panels
for Robert Burns, and Corti himself, his pipe in hand,
his tools cut in granite by his brother
and brother-in-law, and get kissed. And Mary—
named for her mother, loved the fireplace
her grandfather made to stand like an oak, with squirrels,
their cheeks swollen with acorns, squirming in,
and squirrels, almost flying, foraging out,
got sick and died a little girl—*one mortal*
wound of the depth

of twelve inches, and of the breadth of half an inch,
and after
said mortal wound was so inflicted,
Elia Corti, otherwise called Eli,
came into the City of Marble
and there languished —
a slender and affectionate man, his black hair
peaked on the right, parted to the left, the sideburn
cut straight from the ear sticking
out of a formal pose, à la Napoleon, to listen
to the conversation of other Italian
men of his day, gathered for supper
at Paul Miani's, after an afternoon
funeral for a niece, a circle of friends,
some of them Anarchists, some not
breaking, separately, or all at once
to hear Serrati's speech, announced on bills
that passed through the granite sheds
that afternoon, a Socialist
editor and propagandist, some not
crossing the black
iron Granite Street bridge that led
to the opinions of other men,
who cut a stone out of the hills, carved
a muscular arm and hand gripping a hammer
on the face, and cemented it
over the entrance of the Socialist Hall. Inside,
Alessandro Garetto took a chair—
and walked to the right of the door—
straddled it, his arms folded on the back, a firm
toothbrush moustache, a gray cloth
cap, cocked right over a tarry
green cigar drooping his mouth. Friends

of Miani's open the door and empty into two
milling handfuls of sarcasm
and hard looks. The speaker late, several Anarchists
ask for the "priest": "Has he gone out to eat
macaroni?" Corti's
brother-in-law, Fernando, asks Garetto if he
is the lecturer. "Be patient," he answers,
"it is only after seven o'clock." His right hand passing
in and out of his pocket, his lips
moving again, but without sound, as if
he were addressing a lip reader. "Days I wake
with a concentration of fire in me, the center
of my anger a revolving
cylinder in my gut, my father-in-law
curled in a chair
and crippled in the next room, the dry leather
of his breathing blowing coals in me.
The hell of the day I sharpen horses,
blades, while my debts
are the dung falling,
following me into more
debt and flies, this horse's
foreleg bent into my groin
pounding the inevitable next shoe. A second later
it's my adopted daughter wailing or the aria
on my wife's lips. Mari Angelica
Garetto. Locked in the Socialist
Hall crowd, unable to hear
sides, anger waving the air, knives,
a fire or a great noise could rake a path
to the street, the iron
bridge, how it feels
in my hand, they are falling

anywhere; Vocchini
why raise a chair; Movalli
why is your shoe
kicking my belly, and Elia, why?
are you just sitting there, and why do they want!
to hold me." Two shots, and Corti, yelling "Everyone
keep still," falls over backward. Silvino Barr,
smoking a short pipe on the front steps, watched
Garetto open the door, pistol in hand, and John
Payetti met Garetto coming down the stairs with a steel-
blue revolver, and stepped aside, and Peter Trentini,
sure the respondent
is the man he saw from where he stood, sixty
paces from the Socialist Hall, witnessed
Garetto running
south to the railroad track, whether
he ran up or down, whether he relayed
the revolver to anyone, Peter Trentini
didn't know, but he knew
Garetto on the run
held a revolver in his right hand
not a crucifix. Elia,
in his brother's arms, pointed to his belly
and said, "It is here.
It is here." —*until the fourth*
day of October, in the year
of our Lord one thousand nine hundred four,
when Elia Corti, then and there
inflicted, did die, and so
the Grand Jurors upon
their oath aforesaid
do say that Alessandro Garetto
feloniously —impatiently

warmed a police station lacquered
oak chair, Policeman Wood
examining the head (a deep hole
in back, little cuts
on each side) of the respondent at eight o'clock:
Color of Hair: Iron gray; Color of Eyes:
Brown, "all a quiver
and shook"—*wilfully*: when Special
Policeman McPhee, examined by Attorney Hoar,
corroborated
Officer Wood's testimony, he told how Garetto
(watching ants
cross the courtroom floor or the light reflected
off his fingernails) confessed
to him that night that he secured
the revolver weeks before in Chicago.
That there were a number
of women alone on Granite Street,
and a solemn crowd of six
or eight hundred eyes, Officer Wood
was adamant, while Corti, borne
on a litter of arms, was carried
across the bridge, and back
to Miani's—*deliberately*: two hundred men
walk ahead of the hearse, three-quarters of a mile
of carriages trail up the S-
curved hill, an occasional
horsetail swatting a leaf falling. Out of muscle
near the tail of the spine, Doctors
Chandler, Lindsey, and Doctor F.
Ligouri withdraw
a ball that passed entirely
through both walls of the stomach in their hands,

healed, but unable to stand the shock. They
sew it up, cover him, and leave. Serrati in his cell
out of paper, using bar-striped
daylight to write and think, tells his keeper,
"Three sheets
is not enough." His tongue, pushing
on teeth gritting against a frown,
speaks, but without sound, as if
he were lecturing
a lip reader in a subversive chronicle: "He quits
machines. He buries his hammer
with his shovel. He quits tapping
this century and flowers into a granite block
and runs with a Frenchman, Anarchist, Syndicalist, Jew,
Socialist, Italian, and Spaniard, joining
the bones of his voice to the cry of those for whom
injustice is a plague that spreads without
this answer: 'We shall go back
to the factory, to the field, when the capitalists
grant the strikers' demands, and free hostages
kept alive in the disciplinary
shop of the spreading jails
of monarchy into the new world.'" And Giacinto
Menotti Serrati received a mass
of telegrams, one bearing over two hundred
congratulatory signatures. Garetto's portion
of the jail, while his wife, Mari Angelica,
practiced a title role
at the Granite Opera House, has a cage for pacing
in front of his cell or learning English in the near
dark from Clyde Lamb, who possessed a brilliant
tattoo on his thigh of a headless, nude woman
with a heart for a neck, indicating

his mistress. On the other thigh
Clyde himself, designed
holding a stick
in an attitude of bravado
and defying the police: under this,
his sobriquet
printed in green: "Disembowel
Everybody" — with *premeditation* — Occupation:
Blacksmith; Money When Admitted: Fourteen dollars
and eighty-three cents — *and of his malice aforethought* — scar
left calf, and three
vaccinations on left
upper arm — *did kill*
and murder — convicted January 2nd — *contrary*
to the form — discharged
August 4th, 1910 — *of the statute*
in such case made and provided — Schooling:
Common; Clothing: Fair — *and against the peace* —
In Case of Sickness Notify: Mari Garetto, and,
while the Badger & Company ambulance, horse and driver,
makes its way up the Granite-Marble Road under the northern
lights, allow me to present a Dialogue
of Old Friends, followed
by Sam Novelli's Monologue addressed
to no one out of the back of the ambulance
that arrived at the hospital three and a half hours
after Corti was shot, and translated
from the Italian for an American audience,
warned that no refunds will be granted for
this performance if you can't follow
the rotation of the spokes,
the subtitles — *and the dignity of the state* —
Just make sure, Samuel, that they keep Dr. Harewick's

beard away from my wound; he is like an orange pepper
stuffed with rice: he doesn't believe I speak English
and the knowledge that fills his heart
is just the hard grains, cuckolded
by nervous fingers from his moustache into his mouth
into the printed black and white
of his bloodstream; one blond
grain or two pumped out of that farsighted
cold water tap, and you, Samuel, may be carving
my stone in the morning. *Mr. Novelli, you must
keep the patient absolutely silent; it will be after
midnight before we operate. His life, sir, if you
get my meaning, is in your hands. You may speak to him,
but whisper.* Elia,
you musn't speak, but how can I whisper
over that horseclatter! Remember the night the mules
dragged the Burns statue up the hill, and our bellies
heavy with Mary's garlic chicken, and Guglielmo's
grappa. I felt, but my tongue, thick with joy
and stinking of garlic, wouldn't speak such love
for you, for your eye, as I watched you
move around Robert Burns, your hand the final touch that made
    him
live for me. And how your four panels hold him up! A few
lines from the poet, a relief
of his simple beginnings; I especially
love *The Cotter's Saturday Night* — Elia
in a few weeks our moustaches
will be powdered with granite dust, bringing us
to life, and how your Robert Burns plows up the earth!
The ambulance rolled as far as North Granite, and Garetto,
at 9:15, was taken down for Elia to have a look: Yes,
he is the man who shot me. Garetto said, "Look harder,

you make a mistake." And when I,
beside myself, Elia's friend and partner, six
days a week and for the last five years, called Garetto
Assassin, and he called me the only name in his book,
I threw the lantern at him, so he
could see himself as well
as Elia saw him, and went
for Chief Brown's revolver, but he
was too quick
and held me back.

II Mary's Day

Looking away from an oversized
overdue folio of Caravaggio's
madonnas toward the raised outcry of those
'priests, who kicked him forever
out of Rome, after they stole
a hard look at the suspect
in his canvas, then stepped outside
only to find Caravaggio's madonnas
walking the streets under the light–
colored willow of the Renaissance. Maybe
that new young man, Daniel Beavin,
understands: he never charges
me overtime; and I admire
his three-piece charcoal
pin-stripe suit, as does he
the patina aging on my black taffeta
winter stole. He always
has a good word. Hunting for the right
word to say to his father,
he shot an iron deer at thirty paces, the ball
ricocheting back up the barrel, and dropped
such a marvel in the snow
and for the oncoming
years of his life. On the second floor
he unlocked a small library, furnished
with the ambitions of Egyptian royalty, dust
and taxidermy; an S–
curved fainting couch, a roll-top desk,
and shelves of domestic paraphernalia. Hardly

anyone comes here, and there's a photograph
of the Chelsea-Granite Stage
driving around the square. Haw! Get a move on.
Where town elders are a few
professionals whipping
curve-balls into the statue of a kneeling
granite warrior, who has no catcher's
mask, or any character at all criss-crossing
and gouged into his face, whether you press
a nose spot on the one decent
window and squint
or walk outside and look
sideways at his granite sword the sculptor
intended to scare the wits out of pocket mice
and uphold the peace, who cared only for the special
features of the world from the lowered eye
of a drawbridge. I know

you loved the square
leaded window of the opera house, set your stemwinder
to the conductor's pocket watch
high on the church, and would
have enjoyed such heroic sculpture
for the visible
stir it gave the town that gave up its art
to an industry that gave up the town, and I—
living out my years with daughters—
rumor and quarrel, sometimes requiring
the key to the stairs of the opera house, so I may stand
in the horseshoe of the balcony, that peacock
of a window at my back, and hum a little
something from *La Traviata*. Years,
sweet husband, at my age, almost three

times yours, grow back as easily
as the black hair I barbered
off the back of your neck. So, I honestly
must say only thirty minutes ago
I crossed paths with your assassin,
gray and scowling toward the open
market of Milan, his face at sunrise, jealous
still and brooding in scars,
spoiled my day,
only minutes from holding your hand.

Costumes
in the Forbidden City

Costumes in the Forbidden City

I   The Revolutions

At the gate the guard chewed sunflower seeds over Lida
Ivanova's papers, his eyebrow raised
at new factories that began crawling at the hilltop
until they stalled at his perusal
of my baggage. Over which he spat
shells and his permission to climb a wooden
fire escape to the mill superintendent
whose auburn hair was a bunch of beet greens
behind a pock-marked, round intelligence. Back-wash
tender to ring-spinner, climbing a standard ladder
to inspector, and when the revolutions
of the automatic mule started
spinning the boss and his boss
through riders to the warp,
she rose. As the textile machines hummed along
we made our way to the upper floor, where girls on burlap
crossed their legs, trimming the edges of sepia
and off-white piles of lace, harness threads
descending the stairs of a hundred spools
sliced their profiles into a diagonal
stack of hotcakes. The position of an older
woman's fingers pinching thread as it passed
through riders to the warp suggested the mouths
of praying mantids chewing moths, and a green hour-glass
pattern outlined her forehead under a white

babushka. I unstrapped my floodlights, held out my cords
and anxiety to the electrician, that animal, half-
gypsy, yellow-bronze man, who knew, under his
steel wool scalp, that my illumination depended
on black rubber plugs and the ease of his connections.

II

Once an immigrant watchmaker in New York, an active trade
union man and Socialist, sailed home when he got wind
of a revolution, fusing his intuition to the *Americanski*
tempo of big management, and became the head cheese
of all textile manufacturing. I found him sitting
in a cherry-carved relic of the Czar. He made sure I noticed
everyone in the room had calloused hands, nobody
walked the streets with their belts tightened, and he was
sorry he could not provide
momentum for the Manhattan workers'
struggle, or transportation
to the mills because five out of six
cars belonging to the textile
trust were just
"broken."

III Fragment,
and a Photograph of an Old Man

Searching the aisle of magazine creels, the endless
streets of revolving eyes, until I reached behind
clouds of steamy lace and the ever-unraveling
white-hooded girls with oval cheeks
tapering to a demure concentration, digging out
the irregular, moist
knots and slubs, to find
two figures under snowballs of roving, radiating
from medieval spool towers, setting the focus for the tail

of the comet, as it passed from the beam
to the bobbins: over the old man simmering under a skull cap
and a girl wearing a kerchief like a soup ladle, the handle
resting on her spine, and they tended the automatic mule
with a sober expression, while I inspected
the limits of their image in the frosted glass
fitted in the back of the camera bellows. The glass fell
as glass will, and I had to measure off their heads
in space. The fingers spread
and crossing over each other
over the lace crossed my eyes. The atmosphere
between the lenses steamed
my shutter out of whack. The old man
had a toothpick I broke in half
to jimmy the shutter, and with a glass
fragment and a cable release, I composed
all of us, one exposure after another, until

the old man's eyes magnified with tears.
Why does he cry like that, I asked Lida Ivanova.
"He cries only for joy, because you picked an ugly
old fellow and his granddaughter instead of milk-fed
svelte Muscovites he has strained after
all his life, almost."

For the Morning Ascension

The true hallmark of a period is the shape, proportion,
and the details seen as a whole, and all rising from
the idea surrounding the structure.

For all of us dreaming the cottonmouth
lullaby underneath the red and green Chinese
character of the spotlight—ascending the Venetian
blind wrinkles drawn, pocket-to-pocket, across the blue
neutrality of her jeans, and the ground cover
of her upper lip arrested in Turkish
smoke and wine—there are,
before the microphone, Bulgarian village
women in babushkas, men in sash,
and those of us in love
with the evening roll up our sleeves
under raised hands and a congeries of alabaster
white elbows in the Plaka cafe beneath the plaster
death mask of Colonel Rodytis, gone brown
and cracked at the edge of his beard like the groundfallen

leaf of the fragrant oleander. Earlier,
we were just leaving the orchestra
from "An Evening with Nicol," cocksure and balding
genius of the proscenium
palming his eyes—his fingers were octopus
tentacles waving his skull
for an encore—telling us the brass
railing around the pit is above all
the elbow-polished gunwale of a gondola. *Ce ça,*

we smuggle the gondolier among cargo
and onto a semi-private
stall in Lee's Tomb, a Tuscaloosa cigar-
box-shaped country-western bar, and blind pig,
perforated by a spinal
column of booths, back-to-back, in a southern exposure
of North America, where every
turn of the lens and neighborly stranger—Hog Tom

the kidnapper, who made his guests plow furrows, eat alfalfa
flowers and broom,
living in a manger, and Will Purvis, rich kid, his greasy
pinched skull, and green money torch singing
from a pocket, slipped the noose, outliving the locally famous
remainder of his life: pacing
the hardwood of a furnished room in Baton Rouge, or laying
low in the backwood tree house on his cousin's place, just
inside Mississippi, next to the detail of the Holiness
or Hell sect, who were too immersed
burying twins, nearly alive in their mother, to pay
much nevermind to Will in the night—looking up

over the men's latrine at the exposed gray
wrapping of a swamp cooler, looped like the W
in World View into tarry
roof gravel and a star, under which
Florentine Mike, victim
of thieves who drew a straw
map from the tailgate of their four-wheel drive,
pantomimes
an Alabama rabbit season vignette:
a bowhunter
sliding an arrow out of his quiver. We shake

hands, zip our flies, and push the doors out
into the middle of the annunciation
of a woman holding forth: something smoke-
glazed in the curve of her corneal membrane might
have twisted Gabriel, messenger angel,
around her small
depression; and something
like a possible white pea fowl
walking fast through her eyes, is in awe

of the flesh stretched over two
of Degas' women, one
brushing the wings of a tablefly spinning in beer
with the edge of her hand, the other
immersing a forefinger into the tongue of her shoe
under the booth and on either side of John Allison's

flock, thinning over the little bones of his ear that relish
the bearded drummer's oak on steel
rim shots, looking up in a rapid eye
movement from the belly of his snare at Liz
Thomas, who is inhaling swampfire,
tar, and Spanish moss, and sketching hazel into the colored
barscape of her poem on napkins, which is about
when, in the style of a fire department
bucket brigade, we pass the gondolier, shitfaced
and light as helium, back
into the beige

naugahyde of Lee's Tomb, when and where
he swears: not
cooling his toes in the Lagoon of Venice, or navigating
the canal of his basic desires could he ever want more

than this
dream of a dream of a booth or a boat, with and for,
within and from: all of us, dreaming, open our eyes
on the sunlit syllable of the first Venetian
rebel yell, closing the lid
of the humidor. Period

The Traditional Form of Music Is a Bird

for Leon Moshontz

"You must show yourself more human than critical,
then your pleasure will increase." Scarlatti,
on presenting his first sonata

It's 6:30 a.m., October 11th, 1969. Presenting
me waking up between cornstalks cut two
inches aboveground, like a customer opening
his eyes to a crewcut and a shave, wrapped in a sheet,
looking into one mirror into another
over his shoulder at acres of cornstalks
spreading infinitely in both directions. A silver maple
you will never hear from again, breaks
my vision of the kitchen door of a two-story
wearing an asphalt blue shingle bonnet, pinned
with lightning rods. Under which my wife
mutes her snoring with a pillow. There's a legal
yellow pad and me ghostwriting
the life of the Brazilian military, who are too busy

tickling a farmer and his wife with a brace of steel
guitars wired to chairs. In early July a lightning bolt
sent half a speechless silver maple arcing
over the house. Marilyn hid out in the fruit cellar,
while I chased around the yard after peacocks

and waterfowl. The maple presents itself in the negative
yellow and black light of the storm and memory, landing
on the porch and ducks. You can't see from where
we are sitting but a black-
and-white Friesian cow rising tail first
on a winch, her forelegs wired to a mason jar
clattering with hard candy, is a signal
for a belly laugh from the rendering
plant driver, Abe Miller, whose face is the sunrise
hoisting her up. Before the war he lodged
with my great-uncles in Prešov, Czechoslovakia,
who told me Abe laughed in his sleep on wheat straw
scattered on the packed dirt of the dining room,
and escaped with them to the French

Occupation, hunger and the lookout for collaborators.
Because Uncle Manny sent them one sock
and one shoe, eventually they got them. Great-cousin
Hertzke,* the stowaway, came to Cleveland for a wig,
a leg, and teeth, wiped off a meal, and sailed
back to France. This was after my father's spell
in the air force hospital, when he and Hertzke
killed a split fish and onions, chased stewed cherries
and kreplach with tea and seltzer. Hertzke wanted to know,
after a round of blintzes smeared with sour cream, where
is the whore house, and would my father instantly introduce him.†

*Pronounced Hairt skee. Accent on the first syllable.
†Listen, I once asked my grandfather (when he and my father were waiting for a
Sunday morning religious show to become a ball game) if Adam and Eve were
both white, where did black people come from? He passed the question down the
coffee table to my father, who was slowly separating a green cigar from a metal
tube. In the hubbub of my grandfather crushing the cellophane off a package of
Viceroys and Al Rosen smiling at first, he forgot to tell me. So, if you really need to
know where they went that night, ask my brother, who, wearing his Hopalong
Cassidy outfit, had the draw on all of us.

Both of us should pinch our noses, pop our ear drums, wipe
our glasses clean on my shirttail, and look out
ahead of us to the windbreak
behind the barn: no ghost of chicken hawk sails over the trees,
no woodpecker punctuates the corn crib, nor does the barn
swallow or pigeon dive, and there
are no oily-headed grackles along the fence. Much of it
supporting generations of grapevine, interrupted
or entwined with elm, its orange
winter mushroom embroidered branches raised
in benediction under the everlasting
light of the sun, adding itself
to a dying tradition. While a choir of Short-Eared
Critics, and other placental flying animals, hang
by their toes from a branch installed
above it all behind a curtain, giving themselves
an upside-down standing ovation, their wings folded
into an opera cape over a plaid cummerbund. Bravo.
Encore. Bravissimo.

Bondage: For the Olympic Streaker

Buildings are light
and what most distinguish the look in his eye. No profile
of a wife bending over a spaniel, or a parakeet
hooking a finger with its beak
defines
the outline of a man who is not poking an ember
with the thigh bone of gelded lamb,
dodging subpoenas,
or drowned with a shinny stick. For years
he bides his time. Communications
satellites circle the earth, dust
in the eye of the northern sky, and the Montreal
building trades
try to catch up to them. By then, the fad
had passed through sleepy commons, shopping
malls, and the needle-trade
district of Hohokus, Moonachie, and Cleveland Heights. In honor
of the instant amnesia of the world, he bathes
his right hand in stadiumlight, carves
a large circle in the air, and links
five smaller circles
within the perimeter.
Circles are color.
Colors are quicklime,
porphyry, and azurite
and what most distinguish the look in his eye
to the furthermost

sunspot erupting into the lava
flow of his imagination. Never telling his wife
or the men at work
why
he took meals at the site: watching the yellow-capped
engineer and his crew erect
a monolithic TV
screen, and another, surrounded
by his men, measures out the track
around the green periphery. Jim McKay, anchor man,
wearing the soft ABC patch on a yellow
jacket—covering

the final homage to the Olympic runner, leaper, and hammer
thrower stalled in their grand
promenade around the five
interlocking rings of twelve-to-sixteen-
year-old girls—and having
daughters himself, he says
he is appalled at the first
nude Olympian of the modern era spiraling
through the round dance of the hundred
Catholic daughters
of the Québecois provincial government, the thirty-
by-seventy-foot television screen zooming
in on the sudden, glossy, internationally famous, French
Canadian spectator's
pale cheeks (apply
your flesh colors, and do
a little shading underneath) the gendarmes
drape
in a white towel and escort into your dream
of seizing the violet glowing center of the world's

living rooms, not
by the scruff of the neck, or required reading, but merely
by releasing the urge to undress—
before a crowd
of seventy thousand
waving glow sticks in the dark, almost
ready to leave—streak and dance,
go directly to jail
and never get a second chance, or even
a matching grant to support a world
referendum of your fans and protégés: sparks
are everywhere and what
most distinguish the wheels
of a locomotive or the inert volcano
in the distant higher ranges of civilization,
where no one is seen and the mouth alone recorded.

Waltzing Roger's Vision

Celebrations on the Granite-Marble Road

Dr. Peter Harewick of Marble, Vermont,
crossed the Langdon Meadow
crushing dandelions and inky caps
on his way to a meal at Ateo Rizzi's
boarding house. Ateo the astronomer
sleeping it off on the porch swing. On his forearm
a tattoo of two hearts, pierced with swords,
representing a mistress who wouldn't yield except
when threatened with death. Last spring
he climbed the six levels of his roof
to sweep off debris and drop chains
down his chimney, when his broom pushed
into the corpse of someone
dressed in leaves, reduced by winter
into no one. A few months
before, he invented the solariscope
and discovered the sun
has a perennial summer, and inhabitants,
including a forest, red and brown
in the fall, replaced by the living
green of summer in January, whose sister,
Pace, recently divorced
Mr. Christopher Stubbs, the author
and star of Mr. Goldstein, an alembicated
Hebrew character, grasping all
of the humorous characteristics
and amusing situations afforded

by the author's life and experiences. And on
her way from rehearsal to a noon meal of pork
and vegetables, Pace stopped
to watch Mr. Flowers on his knees. You might recognize
the lines in her eyes in sea-polished stones
gathered quickly at the beach, before the tide
washes your new collection and sneakers away, then on
to the big stage of the Goddard Seminary, before
an audience of five hundred
or more, Pace rushed a pack of thirty sophomores
against the freshmen on the stage, at ease,
smashing the president's chair
over his opera hat, eyes black, rough and tumble, and,
you might recognize the border
of her vulnerability when you press a fork
down on the skin of a lima bean, or stop
to watch a young woman
weave a basket around herself. Pace stopped
to watch Mr. Flowers on his knees, his pelvic-
length hair thrown over his face
as a rag, as he scrubbed and spoke
of a Christian way of being,
spit-shining the shoes of the governor, who bent over
and parted the curtain of Mr. Flowers' hair.
To the lines of people milling around
and to the darker episodes
in Mr. Flowers' eyes, that embellished country poems
and horror stories by oil light, the governor
made this announcement: "There is to be an exhibition
of fireworks, and a bonfire
honoring my birthday. The state executives — 'Cracker'
Jack Morgandy, the son of my right hand; Ed Breed, that son of
my left; and Harry 'Boom Boom' Blodgett — contracted

Badger & Company for three hundred fifty rockets with the
    combined
weight of one thousand pounds, like my wife,
who will ignite the Langdon Meadow at eight o'clock. Thirty-six
tourbillions, silver and gold, two hundred ninety shells and bombs
fired from mortars, embracing
aerial exhibition and dragons
breathing over the capital, and, especially
for the little ladies, a flock of flying
ceramic figurines, one thousand
Roman Candles fired in batteries, waterfalls,
and meteors will attack the crowd, while your eyes
are lit by colored fire, a grand
national salute, and prismatic display. The climax
will come during a set piece
of me, your governor at thirteen, climbing
Camel's Hump in lederhosen, encircled
with the words, 'I'd climb a mile of democracy
just to see where it came from,' then little Evelyn
Pitkin will pull a switch, launching
a rocket through a cameo display
of my heart, setting fire to a pyramid
of barrels, six hundred of them, empty and dry,
founded on the material of two
demolished houses, four hundred cords of wood, and twenty men
on twenty ladders, twenty-five feet in the air, will drip
kegs of oil. This fire at its worst
will rise two hundred feet over the marble-robed
goddess of plenty, her feet
planted firmly, and for years to come,
on the egg yolk over the home of our government. And you are
all invited." Meantime, Christopher Stubbs
locked himself and Harewick in Ateo Rizzi's

eating parlor, pulled the official
carving knife out of a ham, rushed Peter, unarmed,
writing notes in a book, and cut him twice,
before the doctor seized a fork, Peter fell,
and Stubbs, turning in the style
of a hammer thrower, swung a lamp
into the beveled edge of a mirror
over Peter, disarmed and quietly bleeding,
watching Christopher
taste a sliver of ham. Looking up
into surgical light, just
able to hear his colleagues, Dr. Chandler
and Dr. F. Ligouri, argue
on both sides of the controversy, while an insurance
executive and a head of state
run around the capital without stomachs,
make their appointments, and survive
on twenty meals a day. Through swinging doors,
twenty paces away, Pace is numb and seated under pipes
overheating the pale green length of this emergency
corridor. A boy enters
holding an undergarment to his mouth, leaning
on the arm of a woman Pace
could never forget. Miss Helen Standish,
lay tutor of the local seminary, better known for the changing
color of her hair, best known
for a short fuse. Pace also knew the boy
had a Seminole grandfather, shot trying to prevent
white hunters from stealing their birds, the delicate
wings of the rainbow destined for the millinery
trade of Savannah and Boston. He made his son,
Bill Woodchuck, promise to refuse the poachers'
whiskey, and fight,

side by side, with the colored runaways. Taken
into slavery, he called himself Fungo Willy, and eventually
moved north on the underground. An Armenian
named Sarafoff steered him to her boarding house.
She broke three eggs into a smoking
black iron pan. Balloons
of egg whites rose in the oil. They married. She gave him
the business, her last name, and a son, who spent
Saturday nights driving an ambulance, and attended
classes at the seminary. One Saturday
morning the Sarafoff boarders opened a few bottles
of Canadian cider, and by afternoon
they were in a fighting mood, had the tiniest
spree with knives and bottles. Willy injured
Boof Shakaloroff, but everyone fell asleep. Much later,
on the street, Boof and his friends colluded:
"Smother Sarafoff and his wife and all the boarders
that get in our way." Special
Policeman McPhee found Willy bent over, cleaning
the oven at four in the morning, and his wife
sleeping it off under the bed.

Miss Standish and the boy joined Pace on the bench.
Miss Standish told Pace what the trouble was:
"I commanded him to put out his smart-aleck tongue;
I took hold of it between my thumb and forefinger.
He's a little too old to be screwing his face
at me, so I took steps in my defense, and even
when his tongue came loose at the roots, because
he jerked his head back, I dismissed the class, and commanded
him to turn around, took off my half-petticoat
to stop the bleeding, and saw the boy through
deserted streets—where are they

41

when you need them—and drove with him in the ambulance.
No bulletin of his progress will be issued today,
and both of us are bound to receive
the indignation of such a place
but there is great
hope, isn't there? for another day."

Waltzing Roger's Vision

I   The Raw Material

Romulus Hush side-stepped through Ellis Island on March
15th, 1902. Changed partners, changed hands, suffered
the evacuation of his name, many an address, investigation
and fire until he hung a shingle in Marble, Vermont:
Waltzing Roger, Professional Ghost — and Free-Lance — Writer,
Ballroom Dance and Graphic Design. Roger fell in
with two Japanese converts at the Marble Assembly of Christ,
doted on by mice and the minister. He followed up
their running script straight down the margins
of their prayers, all translating into military gossip, obtained
through piety and diligence. Disguised as spinsters, these two
oriental poseurs and Roger
waltzed past a recruiting officer toward the ladies' matinee
lecture at the opera house. A speaker appeared
in native costume, the audience
in ecstasy over the delicacy and grace of fabric
overflowing her hands in flight
elusive as the life-line of a snowflake. A clerk
in the gallery agreed out loud there was nothing
like this in stock: how many can she wear at once?
When a half-dozen lay across the lectern, a floor light
illuminated her red fingertips tucking these
into a sleeve, and her lecture
disappeared into the other. For an encore she broke down
the lectern into a case, tossed it with a pinch of salt

over her shoulder into a pouch invisibly sewn on her back,
and bowed into the wing, the applause
falling toward intermission. During which our spies, each
looking into his own eyes at the bottom of a cup,
are listening to Mrs. J. J. Barraby of Middlesex,
a colonel's mistress, confide
in Baroness Stemsel, wife of the magistrate, who believed
"those mysterious pockets go out of their way to conceal
the outward thrusts of the inner self. Don't you agree,
Margaret, that women *en masse* are as spirited
as tea and cookies? Forgery
and grand larceny are out of their league,
but their foothold on honesty is like butter in July, and
their growing inclination toward kleptomania
alarms me. You can see that the average
woman at this matinee is tentative, bustling
to please the men, anxious, self-
centered and deceived. O yes, she is interested alright
in her relationship to things, but the thing itself
evades her. If these potholes in the fabric
are not redressed, our entire sex will step forever
into a social function."

II   Because an Old Mattress Danced

And because Roger was handsomely commissioned the very
next day when his Anonymous Patron desired him
"to design and disperse
an illustrated obituary of a rival
political figure," whose shape in life
a local housewife compared to an old
mattress spring with a leer, Roger inconspicuously
struck up a waltz and out
into the countryside, on a log spinning
on a river, under spiked shoes and a red sash,
slapping hands with asbestos miners in a round dance.
Claiming no style
he tutored a potato patch in a soft shoe, believing
in a rhumba with a conductor of a second-class train.
In overalls, pushing a wheelbarrow, cask, and flag, he insisted
that every postmaster's hand, canceling his name with a stamp,
would bring him close enough
to the wrist of the state, so he could lance it
with his pen and take its pulse. Licked
by dogs, bitten by snakes and the universal
desire to write a book, he contra
danced eighteen miles a day, executed a hornpipe
on a marble block, and a minuette with a quarry worker just
northeast of Rutland. He choreographed
the average length of a word to an inch, allowing
for the curvature of the letters and the earth, the fountain
pen swerving to the west, while this fairly tall
high-stepper with a short beard
and brown eyes, half-a-mouth in a smile, the other

sedate in concentration, leaped
over thirty words before supper. Which he earned
by shuffling the queen
of hearts and her country daughters, taking dimes
from the king and jacks for aluminum postcards engraved
with a poem and very natural scenes. Abused
and robbed eleven times between Manchester
and Woodstock, asphyxiated
over coffee, or rolled down an incline
of wild strawberries, he finagled his pamphlet
distribution after dark, then clicked his stained
red heels toward the stars and the next town.

III Pamphlet and the Greatcoat

Paul Massono, among spectators entertained by a club
of lions and storks, is etched into the cover. Turn the page
and find out how his ambition
to swallow the whole donut cuts off his speech and breathing.
On the third the birds peck and flap. The animals stampede
and leave this sight to providence, who is
punching himself on the back, and driving a silver
spoon down his throat. Nightsticks
beat a path through the finale on the back cover, and
believing the spoon a pistol they bring the show down.
Waltzing Roger has quoted himself
as saying he will deliver himself up
to his publisher soon after
winter leads him around to spring, to the death
rattle of his own
biological metronome. But let's follow
his lead, bowing
his way out of double doors overlooking Lake
Memphramagog, grateful for a Spanish
sausage poached in wine, only to find
his wheelbarrow and all his veteran
possessions had disappeared. What
is he feeling now? What does he think. Only
his manuscript, critically weighted
down with a rock, and a pack rat's final analysis, was game

for a waltz. Roger on his toes, brushed away
the dirt and lifted

the hem of his greatcoat, suspended over the lake
like the monolithic
shadow of a covered bridge. Knock on wood.
Walk on water. And they did.

The Vermont Suicides

The Magistrate Version

Lord Salls is in the toils at last.
By Christ it will be more than time before that scheming
Sarah Bernhardt resurrects his melodramatic
posturing: sporting an opera hat for the prologue,
his lordship
parts the doors of a general store, stogey in hand,
like a man of culture out for his morning.
He doffs his hat and coaxes the general into shooting
the breeze through his majesty's forelocks, so orange
in prisonlight they're outlined with the green
patina of copper. In Act I he wagers
five big ones his collapsible hat is tall enough to swallow
six gallons of the darkest maple syrup in the house, then,
when it has not, he delivers it home over the general's confidence
in his capacity to see what's up. Act II finds the missus
back to back with the general. Lord Salls, helping himself
to the till and stock of a repeater, captures
their attention with a fast one about old bilious
Doc Hamlin and Israel Dubie, the blacksmith. Now this doctor
        leaves
his farm in the hand of providence, and a set of harrow teeth
with the smith, who tells anyone that asks
it was his wife's prize mother
hen pecked out his eye snoozing by the cedar hedge, but you see
this wad between my gum and cheek, if that's tobaccy, then this
        finger
is the pope's nose. Now Doc says he will call for the teeth
"after a little." He does. Counts them like buffalo head
nickels into his buckboard. Dubie reminds him that some

are still hot from the forge. "No matter telling
me that. I guess I know which are and which aren't." And the huffy
old bird drives off without paying. Intermission.
     And now General
and Mrs. Store, before your worldly goods, possessed
with a desire to make the earth a little smaller, join
my troupe of missionaries
waiting outside, let me repay you with the extra-
ordinary secret of the Rosicrucians and the Grand
Masonic, Wall Street, and the light rain over Barcelona.
     You will find
it rings a bell in the three most
priceless things you can imagine: the wheel-turned, glazed,
high-fired ceramic jugs of a nun; the hand-blown, millefiore
crystalline
balls of a priest; and those bluebottle fiddlehead flies.
The final curtain rises with the sun over the uprising
of Doc Hamlin's spurs from their slits in bed, coming
around again with another migrating
bag of teeth, and he says he will call for them
"after a little." Between us, Missus, does a man
with a royal flush pressed against his cheek
beat the nicotine
out of a blacksmith with a full house and a tobacco leaf
plastered lip? He does. But
in casting his winnings into the bowels
of his buckboard, a hot tooth bites flesh
and his mouth opens like the future home
of a Moslem prisoner-of-war tastefully
furnished with a sacrilegious, pink swine's lament. Israel, why
in hell didn't you tell me? Well Doc, as I
recollect, you said, the last time you left in a hurry, you knew
the cold from the hot. Did you, by any stretch of your precious

forefinger skin, run across one? The curtain falls. The police
arrive. Because of Salls' reputation for legerdemain, lest he
disappear by some black-artful prestidigitation,
I've rigged him
upside-down in the confession booth of the wrestling
Parson Tucker, who stands five foot three, one hundred
and sixty pounds, itching in wool stockings to pin
all the bones in his congregation, that have joined
just for a crack at this minister. Quietly approached
one Sunday morning after
communion with a lady contortionist, whose thighs
could magnify a wafer and the tip
of her tongue, fifty times their size, by a quarry worker
who overheard, in his own words . . "that you gave my boy
a lickin' in night school. He says you're a peach, and that
you tied him in a bow, and would be pleased to entertain
any member of our family. Don't get me wrong,
I don't relish this carrying on, but Dominie,
I got a boy you can't throw." Who stepped forward
and confessed: "Lately, Father,
the devil himself has laid hands on me, and if it comes
to a hand-to-hand fight, I want
Parson Tucker on my side and squeezing
the devil into a pretzel." Now the elders
aim their hymnbooks like toadstabbers
at the back of the pews, and when they step around
a miraculous
blood spot in the aisle, they insist religious
training is marching backwards to the good old
days of martyrdom, when excess
of tomorrow slapped its thighs, and everyone,
having something to look forward to, laughed.

Diptych Entitled
All Face the Gold Lady

I   When the story of the Civil War

broke in the papers, Frank
Butterfly, granite polisher,
left the business with relatives,
and marched with neighbors
to the front lines. Where I found him
overwhelmed by a fever, and wounded,
and all hope of recovery
and even the nurse
walked away. But his constitution
broke the fever, rallied
against the wound, and received
a transfer to one of the largest
magazines of the Union Army, where men

on lighter duty were drawing
charges from a consignment of old shells
taken from a peddler at night
traveling by hay wagon
in a southerly direction.

II   The force of the chain

of explosions hurled the shells
of houses, men, and iron window
frames across the Mohawk. And Frank walked
among a light detail of men
from the far end of the island,
where they could smell the reason
a black kettle swayed
over kindling, tired
and toward supper at the arsenal.
And maybe the third
or fourth eruption raised him
above the ranks of officers, stars
against a backdrop of Union
blue shoulders, that comfortably
survive the evening
warmth of a wife
and daughter, with a bedroll
of earth for life, his view of the night
only blocked by an off-
white spruce marker or a chunk of stone.

Quatrefoil

Nikodemon's Daughter

In Times Roman three long-
bearded Jerusalemites
stood together in the marketplace
of a disturbed morning, dusty
and facing the sunrise. Addressing
the populace, they offered to feed
the mouths of Jerusalem for as much
as twenty-one years. Ra phoo el
ben Myer, a gossip, whose lips,
inlaid with a generation of details,
whisper under the flap of his stall
to another, whose ear, a kitchen
garden of orange
and smoky hair, sways in the breeze
of the old news that of the three
refusing to surrender the city, the one
they call Nikodemon gave his daughter
a tall dowry so she didn't need
to stand on her toes, the ankle
straps of her sandals bruising the flesh.
Her brothers lifted her above
a great chest that embraced the fruits
of a commercial life, fashioned
from aromatic shittim wood by Yitzhak
the Chest Carver, who lost his eyes
but not his finely chiseled

and calloused hands, where Dina stood
before Jerusalem and her father, tears
swimming like camels in the babushkas
and mossy
beards of her relations, and kissed his cheek.

The only way

to prevent poverty, Dear Louise, is
to persuade other women that it's no longer
necessary for them to eat
solid food. So says
octogenarian
Baroness Stemsel of Swords Crossing,
Vermont, whose old form,
nearly eleven miles in circumference,
has withered to scarcely three. It was
formerly enclosed by fortifications, and what is more,
Louise, she has formed a club. The members, including
your devoted sister, sign a blood
oath pledge not to eat a thing, except two glasses
of lemonwater at sunrise. The Baroness
has lived years beyond that dipsomaniacal
magistrate, no husband, if you ask me. Before
preventing poverty became her mission in life,
she developed a comparatively
painless mode of putting lobsters in their place, running
a narrow-bladed knife into the tail, third joint
from the terminal fin, the blade slanted irresistibly
downward, severing
the spinal cord, just
as the water boils, and she defies doctors
to demonstrate that she
is less vigorous than any woman her age. "Solid food,"
she swears, "does more harm, and I warn everyone who desires
to join the club,
she will be instantly expelled if she dares swallow
as much as a breadcrumb."

Don't Fast. Don't Steal.

(Jewish proverb)

It wasn't so much the dime novels, the dance hall,
or the gang feuds: my old man was making twenty-five
painting houses, and double that
hitting up the Saratoga track. We weren't trying
for the glory in it, but I'd never
turn back to the old slow
six days a week, scrambling houses
for silver, or canvassing shrubs for fallen brushes,
because: what's life, anyway. I can't die
more than once. Can you? Set yourself up
for a good time. Burn the money! long as it lasts, then take
the medicine
whenever it comes. I used to like
chewing tobacco in grade school: when the others
gave the teacher a surprise, birthday
apple shower, I stole them. Even then
I had a gang. We grabbed marbles off
the playground boys, who weren't as tough, then I
would steal the marbles from the gang, and when they gave me
an argument, I licked them, one at a time.

Hannah in the Tombs

Hannah Elias, octoroon, martialed
into court on a writ, before the turn-of-the-century
and the judge reduced her bail
from fifty to only thirty thousand, is sorry
she is unable to furnish this amount or the clerk
with any personal possessions, but wishes the court
better luck digging up the common
variety of hermaphrodite
night crawlers, lying foot to head in their burrow,
and will remain in tombs after
her examination by the female
square-lipped rhinoceros of New York, who is
with one exception, the largest
living land mammal in Times Roman in the world.

The Death of Two Sonnets, 7/9 of a Sestina, and Uncle Villanelle, and a Sneak Preview of:

I Volunteer Sonnet

Shoestring watch fobs invade Lake Apocrypha, Vermont,
only weeks after they had taken the capital, where thirty-five short
miles away paupers grin and muffle an unrecorded
strain of cabin fever, their eyes an overflowing
cage of egg whites. Even much loved Sir Rodger
Cross, once confidential adviser to the queen
and elected chief of the volunteer fire department,
was photographed introducing a brick
to a pane of glass and stoking a burden basket

with a brood of shoestrings. Days
after he squandered his fortune on the evolution
of watch fobs to be infinitely braided
out of the fire of his private practice, he tarried
on the edge of a chair, on his toes, and hung two

of the sharp, contrasting colors of private enterprise
from a chandelier, twisting them under his chin, like a bonnet.

II

A young man in Marble, Vermont,
thought suicide would rearrange his morning.
One of the great coin collectors
and a conservative on matters of dress
and conversation, he cared even less for the frills
of pressed duck and soirees, or the society of other
numismatists. But his ambition to be known
as a composer overwhelmed his courage, bit the end
of a cigar, spat, and asked an officer
on the bridge for a light, who was preoccupied
with a winter thaw and mud season thundering
over the dam, who said—holding a match
under the young man's chin—"The discharge of a river
is the bulk of water you hear

pouring into the sea
within a given time,
usually expressed as so many
feet per second, and I can estimate by discovering
the breadth of the average rate of flow
and depth of a river at its mouth
and multiplying." Our "young man"
tucked his ornamental
fob and chain in their diagonal slits, tossed
the cigar in the air, climbed backwards
over the balustrade, pushed off,
and disappeared like one of the last great
expeditions into the ancient
smoke and death.

Magnetic Waters

Three spring fed
bodies of water
in the North East
Kingdom of Vermont
impart
magnetic power to steel-
toed shoes, what have you,
and deflect

the needle of a compass.
A sheriff delivered
the gallows contract—
whereon The Lunatic
of North Montpelier
will hang himself—
to Julien, whose last name
was erased by a fire.
When Charlie Miller was a week

shy of sixteen and sentenced
to die, the sheriff, a vein, thick
and climbing the wrinkles on his forehead,
had compunctions about hanging
the boy. He expressed the bulk
of his feelings to Julien,
genius and possessed inventor,
who swore a cancer on his mother

that he would bless Charlie
with an automatic
scaffold, the simplicity
of the thing making the operation

two sure and easy steps: *one*,
the condemned man steps up to the trap
in iron-soled boots and places the rope
around his neck, or not, either way
a weight opens a valve
on a vessel of magnetic water
under the stage, and, step
two, when the vessel empties into another vessel,
the counterbalance operates and jerks

a plug under the trap,
letting the drop fall
and the condemned man shooting
an eternity
of magnetic waters.

The Tale
of the Green Rose

The Tale of the Green Rose

Will-o'-the-Wisp in the North East Kingdom

The young doe in the clearing, the buff-
colored mark of her chin, and her small m-
shaped humid and black nostrils
bruise the nightsoil. Through her teeth
that grind the kelp-blooded vetch, hemlock
bark, and the white-rooted memory of winter, there is
the huffing, communal
whisper of the herd, the buck and fawns still
among the willow
and raspberries, nosing into a slender
bouquet of hawthorn
and Yankee paintbrush, those
bloodspools drying in every
syllable that steps

out of the carriage, as I, like Renoir,
a choirboy "concealed
behind the great organ" alone with his voice
and one with anyone there in the small light, transplant
behind a typewriter the margins
of four lights on a raised double-hung window
above the silver pines knotted into shag
against a dark exclamation of balsam.

A porcupine,
dining alone, bites into the oak-and-pane
apothecary door, unhinged by Pasini Demolition & Salvage,
and a woodcock hen, leaving her eggs
for a tug-of-war between a night crawler and the limitless
undertow of her beak, weave a fisherman's sorry
net of echoes, around the white-throated
sparrow's song that sweeps
this valley under porchlight, as if
they were points of light in a lagoon.

The Amaranth

and cobalt sun climbs two elms, like a juggler
waving sticks and a ball
over a dream: in the pond a beaver
slaps and dives, circling
around the olive-green
two-legged pot, out of which
a chambray work shirt, an eight o'clock
shadow, and a finely etched
chimney exhale smoke into the low
silhouette of a mud-and-stick
island or tepee with a ghost of white cedar
for center pole. At the periphery

I am straddling a fallen elm, while a blue
heron eclipses the sun
becoming pterodactyl
above the copper-bald
crown the fisherman claims is an erotic
airstrip—brown-and-blue-feathered over the marsh
of this dream of former pleasures,
friendship and neighbors: the exhibitionist
beaver trapped, and Barry, deep-
rooted in the sunset, his torso
confused with the reflection
of lilies that drew a bridge
of bodies from the Old World to the New
and swam under it to teach
in an experimental school, walking his creel
and a stringer of rainbows back to his porch,

where a certified letter fabricated
how
he could be laid off after twelve years,
even though I, less
seasoned, would not comprehend it!

＊

I climb the ladder down
out of the sleeping loft, and call to
the life
at her desk. Who overcomes
loss: of our love affair, her marriage partner—
executing chin-ups, in and out
of the closet—or almost
everything painful, who drives over
for a walk on the sponge-cake earth
of the Chickering Bog, who insists that I

don't have the strength to separate
those two: "Take her
bowling, for a beer at The Thrush, what
really counts is your evening with my best
female friend, imported
from a middle eastern bedroom
town on the Hudson." Sliding her forefinger and her pink
thumbnail around the side of my scrotum, she tells me
that the boys, who wear the rubbery faces
of men whose job is killing,
still masturbate with the memory
of Marilyn Monroe in folded linen from the Waldorf,

but
she wonders if I could arrange

passage to the Bay of Fundy (with a railroad
tycoon and patron of the literary arts) for
her folding bed, her husband, and cow.

Between a low cedar hedge and the river
birch that skirts the rocky twist in the Winooski,
we face each other on our sides. Earlier,
with a tractor, winch, and a hand from Walter Smith's
guinea hens, geese, ex-cons, and sophomores,
Duncan Mitchell "Intuitive Engineer" tugged
the fallen galvanized silo cap
up onto the hay wagon painted U.S. PLAINFIELD
in black letters on both sides,
engraved with dried
rural life and dead cocoons—whitewashed
in chicken shit! With a pitchfork

chained to his back, the silver links illuminated
in the sun, the prongs
fanning out over his mossy profile,
he took the wheel like Polynesian
royalty into a float
through the locally famous Fourth of July parade.

She would be there; I
would strut by and say a little
more than hello with my eyes, my heart reaching
into the coffin of my throat, sporting
male colors: a violet shirt, a wide
cowhide with a tarnished, round
brass buckle, and dungarees, blue
and fading into the swarm. She is guarded

on the left by a bald, short Albanian —
with a full charcoal
beard that curls
like his memory for names and faces, loyal
to the bones of the man Deborah lived with and loved
for a third of her life — and Catherine to her right
would arrange
to be there when Tom returned to a nearly
bare clapboard house on his black-
and-silver Kawasaki. Deborah,
to escape their claustrophobic
hold, takes Duncan's hand as it pulls her
onto the float, so
everyone, up from Yonkers, Marblehead, and down the road
could see the ordinary joy of new love kicking
its bare heels in her eyes. We ran

into each other near the fairground
stalls, where she was holding
Hannah Mitchell's hand, the only one in town
without an opinion, where friends from both lives
ride motorbikes, blow glass, dip their hands
in pans of developer, split hairs
and kindling, dissolving into the dark spinach
shade of an Independence morning, holding foam
cups to their chins, steaming
polarized lenses. We break

from the nine-headed, two story loaves of sourdough
and puppets; the silver
pockets of gossip spit on the green; Korshak's
tawny spectres in harness
tug-of-war with Bartlett's mules, while we,

on our sides behind the hedge, could have knotted our shoes
together, over our shoulders, crossing the river twice
to my Chevrolet; instead, we brushed
what we could off our clothes,
and ungainly walked our grass-stained
elbows back through this uneven, midsummer's dream...

We met at breakfast: I was holding
forth in the northwest corner. My subject
grew wild and poisonous beyond a self-made
house framed out of rough-sawn boards, a clear
plastic sunroof over the kitchen
climbing toward the waves of a stainless-
steel roof surrounded by lime-green tamarack

with their tight little cones. To my right, Tony,
a carpenter, stabbed a sausage with a fork,
while Alice, mother
of nearly three appetites, scouted
for bits of yellow egg tangled in his beard,
and watched his tobacco-stained finger scrape the air
for that passionate word
stuck between his tongue and
an inherited tooth bent inward. She appeared
in the southeast, barely awake, not late

enough to miss a
spotted griddlecake, a lacquered wave
of bacon, and the forehead
of the carnelian orange-
bearded, medium-tall, skinny man next to her—streaked
violet

and aquamarine under the ruptured glass lamp—
frowned, and they were introduced as Tom the glassblower
and Deborah the sculptor. Sniedze, a Latvian weaver,
reached across the equator for a brown crock
of whipped butter and said
she loved the wild mushrooms in the mixed forest
behind her farm, her calloused fingers
steaming over a coffee mug, and listening
to me chant *Armillaria*
mellea, Amanita muscaria. Sniedze replied, her hair
woven into vines, that honey mushrooms
are fall mushrooms, and this
was not even July. Deborah joined
our walk, and Tom *would* but he

was met at the screen door by a protégé
who blew milk-white, shaded
glass revolvers, shouldering
a Machiavellian dagger-shaped punty that would gather
from the iron pots
blooming on the furnace floor
fingers of milky opaline that they
would embed within, and overlay, the red
foot of the mouth-blown goblet
joined to the blowing iron rim; then,
after he warmed another punty, and thrust it into the bottom
of the webbed foot, she filed the lip into a jagged edge,
broke it
away from his pipe, balanced like
a swan roasting on a skewer, then Tom,
flaring the lip with a tong, pressed the shoulder
with a pinsnip: then, al-

together, driving it home into the glory hole, after which he gave it, like a sleeping flamingo, to the infinite disregard of the annealing oven.

Ambassador Lanes

Kneeling over the bean row, your back to the river,
the breeze throwing your black,
shoulder-
length hair across your eyes, you groom
and prune a bush. Catherine — your live-in
lover's part-time mistress in another room furnished for a queen-
sized mattress under your ceramic
relief on the wall and the memory of the more or less
anonymous corpse of your friendship buzzes
the blue-flowered rosemary on the window sill.

She refuses
our invitation to drive anywhere we please
after a meal of carp
roe and summer onions cut
on the diagonal. Plenty of wine, and you both
whisper over the length of my thumbs, follow the ravine
up the back of my neck . . . At Ambassador Lanes we slide
three fingers into the swirling red
and black holes: Deborah's throw

pulls
straight into her father's twisted wire
furniture factory above the
chairs burning to the ground
floor of bankruptcy and welfare. A split. Her mother
loses herself in a sequence of other men. I hook
into the gutter, my right arm and leg arcing
upward into the new stone age

statue of a messenger, who, having swallowed
courage, in the face of ten
enemies, was bringing it up, balanced
on one shoe dyed the purslane
colors of memory . . . *the smoldering*
beds of cedar shingles, hose,
and firemen percolate on the evening news after brother Jeff
and I drive home from the shortest
day of summer at the retail yard. At The Thrush
we lick salt off a shared
Margarita, and the cobweb
from our private cellars of purpose
and desire, under the green-striped canopy;
under the stars
bleeding into the rain, we run for the bucket
seats of the Chevrolet. In the driveway (your man in the house
just a lamp glowing through the window shade) we touch
hands, and Deborah, luna moth
against the windshield, says "No one
should feel remorse. Come at seven
on the second of July. Tom will be off
blowing glass at the Bennington Fair."
We kissed. She threw her arms like coral snakes

against the glass, her fingers opening
into the white tentacles of the sea anemone,
and said
"Suck my blood." In love, I drove
down Eva Foster Road, where a doe in my headlights,
missing an ear, bounded out of a cornfield
and into the ferns, while Deborah walked back
into an arrangement of arms, her eyelids like
skin-divers swimming into the aquamarine

atmosphere of solitude, knowing
that night, when Tom reached for her, she
and I would be elsewhere, and occasionally
watching Tom in the clear, unsympathetic dark.

A Glass of Burgundy

The powder-blue boxer shorts fly out the window: this
is dawn unraveling
our several nights rowing the porcelain tubs of The Windmill
Arms, The Doll House Hotel,
and The Do-Drop-Inn. A French-Canadian trucker,
a ceremonial pipe-feather that ensnares
the sunlight behind the cab swerving
on the right, shakes an orange-
and-green eagle on a fist, throws it into neutral
and screams *Vive la France*, driving us
into the left shoulder of another
conversation: at the beaver pond under the lime-yellow

light gashing the foliage, we clamped
a log between our legs; your bitterness,
like fields of salvage, the mounds of sea gulls

picking it clean, explained that Tom
littered the house with students, and other
androgynies, limbo-walking from the screened porch

to the kitchen, your privacy and half-a-room to squeeze
clay into the torsos and facades of other centuries
a premium
he couldn't afford, your ambition the clear
orange lacquer of embarrassment. A size 34
arm around your waist, you spotted
the exhibitionist beaver climbing over his intuitive
engineering to bring a river

birch to a point. And I,
having seen through a knothole in your words
something so large that it could not be traced without appearing
surrounded by the outline of my marriage, buried a year ago
in a glass of burgundy, its opaque surface now marooned
in shadow. And the light
breeze over the pond passed through the room
papered
with mica-thin poplar leaves, where
we took a shortcut the evening before,
and you climbed the ladder down, removing
yourself from the loft and summer trappings: shorts
and a chartreuse tie-dyed affair climbing to an orchid
double knot, marking
the equatorial latitude of a suntan. Joining you, we look away

to the offerings of pine: bronze-and-ivory-
filigreed cones, inches from the complementary
reflections on the sill
around the L-shaped ottoman, and connect our birthmarks
like constellations
upon the thick and scratchy blue triangle of a white rug's
shifting currents: first, I shrivel like a snail
under the tap of a shoe, then
you become the air-dried
plumage of a waterfowl; and then
you step out of the shower, white leaf draped
around a sugar beet, into a house in the woods
without shades, night, and all the lights
of every window a portrait of you
and me, and the moon, sliding
across the skylight, illuminating the white fingernail
under your eye and your surprise,

seeing yourself turn an argument
against marriage into an argument for
the moonlit movements of deer. Their way
through the back clearing. The moon
lifts in silence, filling the window
over the black iron stove. You break the vigil. The deer
twitch their ears.
The deer leap. You are sure
if you took a husband, it must be
someone who could listen
in the dark for hours without fear.

Summer Constellations

She pinched a daydream of blackflies
under the house on piers. We sprawled with the panic grass
around the gelatinous brown-
and-cream-rimmed cups of mid-July—
humidity, dead bees, and moss
circling away under clouded
butterflies along the concrete pillar. An intensive
specialist, she applied

thumbs to the rawhide
knotted in my tailbone; her curling
dark Mediterranean hair fell on my shoulder blades
pressing on to the chicken pox
crater, where my eyebrows
like the black pearl
handles of dueling pistols, crossed, straining to hear

Deborah, her sister, through the floorboards.
Tom, at the other
end of the line, eventually
made headway into her tolerance
for the techniques of blame and stress, offhanded
and sarcastic, until she felt herself
flaring up like sailfish into the vengeance

of insulin; floundering
in the air, which caves in, coming back
out of breath—crying. Having promised
her and ourselves that we could hold

back, but close enough under twelve tons
of plexiglass and western
red cedar, we crawled out into handfuls
of wood sorrel and morning glories
trailing up the porch, where Deborah, her knees
tucked into her neck, her fists like milkweed
pods crammed against her eyes, was
about to burst. Tom arrived

moments after we left for the neon
arrow of the Jockey Hollow Motel,
broke a knife
between his fingers, and, at a still moment,
he put his foot through the louvered
pine door, leaving Cynthia
in the deneivehosture of a porcelain bowl, her belly
turning the fear and cereal.

Of Another Life

We took a room with moss rose
wallpaper and a balcony view above the lobby,
a fairy ring of perch washed up and spaced
four feet apart, like sentries
guarding the lake. A tap
at the door and the embarrassed
voice of a girl asked that we pull
the curtain inside the stall. That evening, we poked

at fat herrings, chopped and swimming on their sides
in sour cream, then washed down in dark ale.
Staring
off into the knotty pine
images of Rembrandt's old men pointing their gnarled
storybook thumbs at children in stocking caps
floating out of the rain-
stained ceiling, we joined them in a grand

promenade around the lounge
chairs and ottomans arranged
like a newspaper labyrinth, where a silver-
haired gentleman bites into a tortoise-shell
cigarette holder, twisting
The Montreal Star into a washrag. On the outskirts
a dowager pressed a diamond
solitaire to the side of her nose. By the side
of her willow rocker, and under our room, a dark, irradiating
ectoplasm, like an overturned Russian cathedral,
watermarked

the red carpet. Outside,
a cat went from one fish to another, surveying the losses
of the House of Denmark. We walked stones
across the water; the moon cut the corner off a cloud
floating in the lake, the best throw
spinning *still* across it.
Before it sank, we might
as well have chased the cat, or given ourselves,
with the Isabella moths, to the coming
severity of winter.

Three things were perfectly clear: the formal Dane
had powdered the sickle-
shaped bags under his eyes
with a red diagonal stitch; confused
by the current passing between us, he didn't charge
for the herrings that had choked in ice; and we
were afraid that all our concoctions, whipped
in fever and without sleep, would evaporate
after American customs, and with the dew. Stopping
for the expected
search through the ashtray, we lost
ourselves in unfamiliar back roads overhung with the jade-
green finery of mid-July, afraid
even to sit on a rock and eat a sandwich,

because the man she left
the "Tom,
I'm going away to think awhile" letter
had a temper, the killing arts tucked
under his sash, and having lived together for nearly
nine years, they kept
their short flings from each other, the loose keys

in their pockets, but they came
together with the international
diplomacy of alley cats, and when

one morning, Tom walked downstairs, and split open
her cheek, just
under the eye, with a dewclaw,

she tried, hysterically, all
ninety-three pounds of her, to take him back.

The Russian Hour

I caught you: eating
snap beans as long
as Tolstoy's fingers, out from under
his muslin; turnips, albino white;
wild pheasant; and not your first
humid succotash. The laundromat

I was calling from was your
native stamping ground in the North East Kingdom:
moat of poverty, mud palace, blood on snow. You were about
to leave Writer's Mecca,
Iowa, for Athens, Ohio; climb three flights
and teach on a hill; have your child

again, and a second wife, a poet, whose words
radiate like the nicotine gold
flourish of your right thumb under
keroselight; she took you for drives along a clear
tributary of the Hocking River, a ladle
handle scooping up into a cave, over which
a spray cools the air above
her blond hair fanning out on the water, while the three
of you bathed, chewed on the altogether
round and peppery leaves of watercress,
wading up the stream to tease the big-mouthed
chubs and suckers. By then

we wouldn't speak to each other
for the fourth time in our lives: like spittle
on a shard of pottery emerging

from a mound of ash, a part of me
would offend a part of you—between us we shared four wedding
ceremonies alone with our wives—but I began this page
calling you away from supper
to say I'm in love but overturned by all the harm
that's scattered in and around us: our friend
in Montreal takes his Demolition Derby
jacket out of the closet, where his child, wife,
their refrigerated
vitamins, and their zip-lock bag of yeast
eat the door handle for breakfast. Deborah
has been living with another man: in 3 states,
5 towns, and for 9 years. I met her
at a morning feast, took her along
with a Latvian Penelope
to a mixed forest. Deborah was thawing
squid for the deep fryer, for Tom
and me, if I *would* come. Tom was scraping silver
off the marver
well into a sunset, and so this small

figure of a woman—who might have been a Daughter
of the American Revolution, a Mediterranean
street vendor, or the portrait of a powdered odalisque
at the Palace of Versailles—sat me down
in a living room wrapped
with earth-colored clay, knotted metal
and satin rattail. She
opened her leather portfolio of photographs
across my lap to a ceramic long ship tattooed
with industrial gears and the fragments
of kitchenware exploding out of the spheres
across a page to the white stoneware
and linen mop-bodied quadruped,

a crustacean stepping
out of a prehistoric assembly line, her eye
for the abstract and too real, believably
culled from the ancestral
memory of gold and red
breads braided into yards
of sweatshop gaberdine flung
across the mud walls of Poland
to the needle-trade district of New York
and captured in clay for any dreamer with an eye:

for a highly textured
figure pulling the cords of my
memory through the clear, convex
corneal membrane, just
as an Indonesian faith healer's fingers pass through the living
walls of the belly. . .

Tom walked into the scene of my
fingers stirring in the burial
ashes of her low-fired wall relief. We shook
hands and cheese over garlic butter, and green
tentacles of parsley, while our conversation glided halfway
up a hill. Deborah uncovered a box
of her father's letters, written
out of anguish and bankruptcy, the slow dissolve
of marriage, and the belief that his failures
would smear his children, and anyone
who touched them: Tom
picked up his fiddle, crossed the room, and sat
the evening out. Even when
the life of the party
appeared and joined our meditation on a man who would curl
up on a couch, after a meal, one hand pinched

between his legs, fall asleep, and mumble: son
of a bitch, son of a bitch. Still

watching the furniture factory smolder in coals, or,
having walked the frozen Hudson to the two-story
in West New York, he is just
unlocking the door
to: no wife boiling milk, or five
children screaming around the machine-
twisted wire furniture that he designed
before a crusade of legal battles
led him into the present, when his playboy
brother wills him: a fabric store in Miami underneath a velvet-
red apartment complete
with a garden on the roof. I saw that Tom
and Deborah's marriage had taken on the ritual of ivory-
and-black keys falling like the willing
resignation of martyrs to a waltz
in ragtime, or was I
hypnotized. Steven, what

would you do
if you were leaning against the pale hospital
walls of this laundromat
in my boots? *I'd take off my pants, pinch my nose,*

and jump while the water's warm, while the days
are as long as our friendship. Congratulations,
and marble fauns,
and my love to your Deborah . . .

A Note About the Author

Roger Weingarten was born in Cleveland, Ohio, in 1945. He attended
Goddard College and the graduate writer's workshop at the University
of Iowa. In 1973 he was awarded a Creative Writing Fellowship from
the National Endowment for the Arts, and in 1974 an individual artist's
grant from the Vermont Council for the Arts. He directs, and teaches
in, the creative writing program at Arizona State University in Tempe.
He is the author of two volumes of poetry, *Ethan Benjamin Boldt* and
What Are Birds Worth. He and his wife, the sculptor Dina Yellen, divide
their time between Arizona and Vermont.

A Note on the Type

The text of this book was set in film in a camera version of Bembo, the well-known monotype face. The original cutting of Bembo was made by Francesco Griffo of Bologna only a few years after Columbus discovered America. It was named for Pietro Bembo, the celebrated Renaissance writer and humanist scholar who was made a cardinal and served as secretary to Pope Leo X.

Sturdy, well balanced, and finely proportioned, Bembo is a face of rare beauty. It is, at the same time, extremely legible in all of its sizes.

Composed by Photogenic Graphics, New York, New York.
Printed and bound by The Haddon Craftsmen, Inc., Scranton, Pennsylvania.

Typography and binding design by Karolina Harris.